Kid YouTuber Because Obviously

By Marcus Emerson

ALSO BY MARCUS EMERSON

The Diary of a 6th Grade Ninja Novels
Diary of a 6th Grade Ninja
Diary of a 6th Grade Ninja: Pirate Invasion
Diary of a 6th Grade Ninja: Rise of the Red Ninjas
Diary of a 6th Grade Ninja: A Game of Chase
Diary of a 6th Grade Ninja: Terror at the Talent Show
Diary of a 6th Grade Ninja: Buchanan Bandits
Diary of a 6th Grade Ninja: Scavengers
Diary of a 6th Grade Ninja: Spirit Week Shenanigans
Diary of a 6th Grade Ninja: The Scavengers Strike Back
Diary of a 6th Grade Ninja: My Worst Frenemy
Diary of a 6th Grade Ninja: Beware of the Supermoon
Diary of a 6th Grade Ninja: Suckerpunch

The Secret Agent 6th Grader Novels
Secret Agent 6th Grader
Secret Agent 6th Grader: Ice Cold Suckerpunch
Secret Agent 6th Grader: Extra Large Soda Jerk
Secret Agent 6th Grader: Selfies are Forever

The Kid Youtuber Novels
Kid Youtuber
Kid Youtuber: Hungry for More
Kid Youtuber: The Struggle is Real

The Ben Braver Novels
The Super Life of Ben Braver
Ben Braver and the Incredible Exploding Kid
Ben Braver and the Vortex of Doom

The Recess Warriors Graphic Novels
Recess Warriors: Hero is a Four-Letter Word
Recess Warriors: Bad Guy is a Two-Word Word

Other Illustrated Novels
Middle School Ninja: Legacy
The Dodgeball Wars 5 Book Collection
The LOL Collection Volume 1
The LOL Collection Volume 2

Visit MarcusEmerson.com for more info!

This one's for Finley...

Emerson Publishing House

Book design by Marcus Emerson
Art created digitally in Clip Studio Pro.

EPISODE ONE:
THE BIGGEST AND BADDEST OF DEALS

SEASON FOUR OF KID YOUTUBER STARTS...

NOW.

104 VIEWS   127 FANS

What's up, internet? Davy Spencer here, back with the most amazing season premiere in the history of ALL season premiers ever! Now, I know I've said things like that before, but this time I promise it's true because this time I've got something ABSOLUTELY, POSITIVELY MIND-BLOWING right behind me.

It's something I discovered in the woods behind my house over the weekend. Something that's gonna rock the faces off every person on this planet.

Something that scientists are gonna be, like, "Whaaaaat?" and then pay me boo koo bucks just to LOOK at.

I don't know HOW this thing got back there, or WHERE it even came from, but those details don't really matter.

What matters is that I, Davy Spencer, will go down in history as the first human being to have his own...

PET DINOSAUR!

GUYS, ARE YOU SERIOUS? I CAN **SEE** THE ZIPPER! AND ALSO YOUR **FACE.**

Look at that thing! It's, like, 2-stories tall and as long as a school bus! Peep this – on Saturday, I was hanging out in my backyard, totally doing lawn work like my dad asked me to, when suddenly, BAM! This Tyrannosaurus rex stomped up to me outta nowhere!

At first, I was scared because IT'S A FLIPPIN' CARNIVOROUS, DINOSAUR. But after it didn't eat me, I started petting it, and the two of us hit it off instantly! I tamed him, taught him tricks, and even named him "Bixby!"

NO, DUDE, MY NAME IS **DINO-MINO!**

C'MON! NOW HE'S TALKING??

Bixby is easily the coolest pet I've ever had. You know how some dogs take forever to learn new tricks? Well, Bixby figured things out right away. I've already taught him how to fetch, how to shake, and even how to tell a joke!

Oh, right, I forgot to mention that Bixby can also talk.

THAT'S how smart he is.

So, not only is he the last dinosaur on Earth, but he's also the last TALKING dinosaur on Earth, so... two birds with one stone... I think. I dunno, that probably doesn't mean what I think it means.

Anyways, yeah, NASA's gonna go NUTS when they see him.

I've already sent them an email about Bixby with pictures and videos and everything. I haven't heard back from them yet, but I'm hoping this video will get their attention.

3

In the meantime, I'll just be chillin' over here with my new pet dinosaur, and would you look at that? It's feeding time!

4

EPISODE TWO:
FOWLIN' AROUND

I'm sure there's one out there somewhere, but it's probably not in my backyard. All I've got are rabbits, squirrels, and an owl that apparently has some very important things to say ALL night long. Too bad I don't speak BIRD.

Anyways, life is pretty normal around here. I'm not an internet rock star yet, but I'm still trying. I mean, I've got lots of Fans, so that's pretty cool. You're keeping me busy with all your video suggestions, so thank you for that!

So, this week is picture week at my school, Wood Intermediate. Photographers have their stuff set up in the cafeteria and will be taking photos every day during lunch.

My picture isn't until Friday. I wish it were sooner, but in a school full of students, SOMEBODY'S gotta go last, right?

No big deal. That just gives me plenty of time to experiment with different kinds of hairdos.

You see, school pictures are more important than you think. Students are forever immortalized by their photo in the yearbook. Twenty years from now, when somebody takes a stroll down memory lane, they'll open a yearbook and see a picture of me, Davy Spencer.

So, why take a lame picture when it can be NOT lame? This is the year I started my YouTube channel, so this year's picture needs to SHOW that!

And what better way to show that than with my hair?

And with all the activity in the cafeteria with photographers and stuff, I also had the brilliant idea of making a viral video during lunch while everybody was there.

That way, they'd have a story to go with my pic, like, "Oh, yeah, I totally remember when Davy did that awesome thing during picture week!"

Now, I know what you're thinking... just SAYING I'm gonna make a viral video DOESN'T make a video go viral.

No, I figured that out back in season 1. But this time is different. I'm older, more experienced, mature. And I know exactly what I'm doing. You see, I'm gonna take SOMEBODY ELSE'S video that went viral... and I'm gonna recreate it.

YOU MEAN YOU'RE GONNA RIP IT OFF?

NO, I'M GONNA **RECREATE** IT!

YEAH, THAT'S JUST A FANCY WAY OF SAYING YOU'RE GONNA RIP IT OFF.

Fine. MAYBE I'm ripping the idea off, but it's all good cuz I'm gonna give the original artist credit for her work!

Actually, I HAVE to give her credit, or I'll get in trouble since the original artist is Krissy, my baby sister.

Back in season 1, Krissy ganked my camera and filmed a video of herself and her dog, Bo-bo, having a tea party in cowboy outfits.

In case you forgot the video, here's a clip...

Mom uploaded that to YouTube, and it got over a million views overnight, making her an instant star on the interwebs.

Krissy nailed it and she wasn't even trying, while I'm over here busting my tush to make videos every single day!

But then I had a thought – why don't I just RECREATE the video that launched my sister's career? If it worked for her, then it'd work for me!

So, my plan was to dress up like a cowboy and have a tea party with an animal, but not just ANY animal... A CHICKEN.

Okay, wait.

Let me back up and explain... Every single school in the world has a mascot, right? A bulldog or a Viking or a tiger or lion or a knight or whatever, you know what I'm talking about.

Well, Wood Intermediate also has a mascot.

And it's a chicken.

Like, for real.

And Miss Gymalski, our retired Olympic weightlifter from Austria, doesn't let anybody forget it, but I think that has a lot to do with her aggressive school spirit.

And because we're the chickens, the school's Future Farmers club is allowed to keep a real live chicken in a caged off section of the school courtyard.

Her name is Pompom and she's literally a big fat hen.

DANG. THAT IS ONE GINORMOUS CHICKEN.

bok... bok...

Kids love her, which is probably why she's so big. The Future Farmers bring her into the cafeteria (in a cage, obvs) during lunch and charge a quarter to feed her. Having "fat chicken joke" throwdowns around her has sort of become a thing, too.

THAT CHICKEN'S SO FAT, SHE HAS TO PUT A BELT ON WITH A BOOMERANG!

THAT CHICKEN'S SO FAT, I TOOK A PICTURE OF HER LAST CHRISTMAS AND IT'S STILL PRINTING!

THAT CHICKEN'S SO FAT, HER BELLY BUTTON GETS HOME 15 MINUTES BEFORE SHE DOES!

Anyways, that was my plan – to dress me and Pompom up as cowboys and film us having a tea party together.

Pretty easy, right?

So, as soon as lunch started on Monday, I changed into my cowboy outfit that I brought from home, and I just gotta say – I looked pretty SLICK in a cowboy hat. It's not an accessory that many fellers can pull off, but there I was, killin' it.

Chuck, Annie, and Fergus already set up a table for the tea party in the cafeteria, so all we had to do was get Pompom out of her cage, which wasn't gonna be a problem because the Future Farmers take her out ALL the time.

When me and my friends went to her cage, she was in there, doing whatever chickens do, roosting or whatever.

I'd never held a chicken before. The last one I saw was when I went to a farm a couple weeks ago, but that one tried to kill me, so it doesn't count. I guess what I'm trying to say is that... I wasn't exactly sure how to pick Pompom up. Her cage wasn't locked, so the first thing I did was open it.

After the cage was open, Pompom just sat there, staring at me. She wasn't spooked or anything, which, I'm gonna go ahead and say, was a good thing.

We held a quick thumb wrestling match – loser had to grab Pompom. Of course, I lost, but only because I had the disadvantage! Chuck's thumbs are like mini body builders from all the videogames he's played, Fergus' grip is fierce from rolling his wheelchair all the time, and Annie just straight-up cheated.

Like always, I was the guy who had to get his hands dirty, and I was running out of time.

Lunch was almost over, and I still had a video to make.

I just had to do it.

Don't think about it, just do it.

So, I stuck my hands into the cage to pick up the fat hen who, up until then, had been as calm as a sleeping baby. But that all changed the second I touched her.

At that point, everybody in the lunchroom was trying to see what the heck was going on with the screaming kid whose arms were stuck inside the bird cage.

Sure, it was attention, but was it the kind of attention I wanted? They say there's no such thing as "bad" attention.

No, wait, maybe they don't say that.

Anyways, everybody watched, but nobody helped.

And THAT'S when things went from BAD to WORSE.

HOW IS THIS POSE EVEN POSSIBLE??

Annie screamed.

So did Chuck and Fergus.

So did everybody else in the cafeteria.

Pretty much every single person in there screamed.

Maybe Pompom was scared, or maybe it was revenge for all the times she had to sit in her cage and watch everybody eat chicken nuggets during lunch.

Everyone ran for the doors. Everyone except me and my buds, who were too busy trying to catch Pompom to put her back in her cage.

When all the students and teachers were safe in the lobby,

they slammed the doors shut behind them, trapping us inside the cafeteria with the bird.

It was a little weird that none of the teachers were helping, but whatever.

YEAH, I'M NOT PAID ENOUGH TO CATCH CHICKENS.

Anyways, for an overweight bird that couldn't fly, Pompom had some serious moves!

She was like some kind of ninja-mutant-monster chicken, turning on a dime and scurrying under tables while shrieking her tiny, yellow beak off.

At last, the four of us had her cornered.

But our mistake was thinking that SHE was the one who was in danger...

Okay, Pompom didn't actually say that. I just dubbed some audio over the video. Pretty cool, huh?

But I guarantee that bird was thinking that because when the four of us dove after her, she went into full beast-mode, clucks clucking and feathers flying. She blasted right through us, hopped onto a table and tore across the top like a freight train, leaving a path splattered food and spilled milk in her wake.

All the four of us could do was watch as Pompom beelined toward the cafeteria doors, which were thankfully closed.

That's when the fat hen fluttered her pointless wings, getting just enough air to slam her body against the long, aluminum crossbars in the middle of one of the doors, which then TOTALLY swung open for her.

So... yeah... chickens are pretty smart.

I sprinted after her, but everybody OUTSIDE came flooding

back INSIDE because of Pompom. It took forever for me to squeeze through the crowd, but it didn't matter because when I finally did... Pompom was already gone.

EPISODE THREE:

. . .

87 VIEWS   125 FANS

So, yeah...

THAT happened.

All I wanted was to make a viral video of myself having a cowboy tea party with a real live chicken without the whole thing blowing up in my face!

WAS THAT TOO MUCH TO ASK FOR??

Anyways, I wish I could say everything turned out fine and that somebody caught Pompom right afterwards and put her back in her cage and that rainbows were shimmering and unicorns were dancing and the universe was perfectly balanced the way Thanos wanted it to be.

But I can't.

Cuz that didn't happen.

Instead, every single person in the cafeteria narked on me. To be fair, it WAS my fault.

I mean, there's video evidence and everything.

GUYS, C'MON! I'M NOT PRETENDING I DIDN'T DO IT!

And I don't feel great about it.

Pompom was running around somewhere in the school, probably scared. Maybe a little angry. Maybe hungry. Sleepy. I dunno, I'm not a chicken!

Anyways, the cafeteria was absolutely wrecked. Chuck, Annie, and Fergus had to help clean up for aiding and abetting me. I really hoped they weren't mad. I mean, they DEF weren't happy, but I'm sure they preferred to be right where they were instead of with me.

OH. FOR. SURE.

I didn't need to help clean up the mess. In fact, I wasn't anywhere near the cafeteria, but that wasn't a good thing.

Instead, I was on the other side of the school, sitting in Principal Hawkins' office. He was upset, but not angry. He didn't even yell. He was just concerned that Pompom could've gotten hurt, or even worse, one of the students could've gotten hurt.

I asked if I was gonna get detention or suspended or expelled, and he said, "No" to all of those. Man, was I lucky or what? I mean, yeah, losing Pompom was bad, but at least I wasn't in as much trouble as I thought I was.

NO, NO, NO. DAVY'S IN A LOT OF TROUBLE.

Then Principal Hawkins told me to go to Room FN-1027 on the second floor. He said sitting in detention wouldn't be a productive use of my time, and that he had a better idea for me, but he said it in an evil villain kind of way, which gave me goosebumps.

And right before I left, I asked him what was in Room FN-1027.

All he said was...

EPISODE FOUR:
THE SECRET ROOM

NORMAL SCHOOL ROOMS HAVE NORMAL NUMBERS, LIKE ROOM 1 OR ROOM 2.

BUT SECRET GOVERNMENT FACILITIES HAVE ROOMS LIKE FN-1027.

99 VIEWS   132 FANS

What's my school hiding in that room?

Was it some kind of secret laboratory where alien creatures dissected human students?

Was there some kind of portal to an alternate reality in there where my evil twin lived?

Or was it a secret government facility where they recruit kids and turn them into super soldiers like in Halo?

Honestly, I was hoping it was the second one.

Because how cool would it be to meet the evil version of myself?

Evil Davy would try to fight me at first, but then he'd realize we'd have more fun if we were friends instead. Can you imagine all the crazy YouTube videos we could make?? We could pull all kinds of crazy pranks as twins!

I went up to the second floor to find Room FN-1027. Didn't take long since it was pretty much right next to the stairs.

The door was shut and had no window to peek through. There was no label on it either, like, "Maintenance Closet" or whatever. It was just a plain old door that was painted the most boring color gray in the universe probably so nobody would ever think twice about it since that's where THEY kept their portal to the alternate reality.

I knocked.

No answer.

Total silence.

I'm not gonna lie — I kinda got myself all worked up at what could've been in that room. An itty, bitty part of me might've even been scared.

But I couldn't leave. At least, not without trying one more time, so I could be like, "Yeah, I knocked a ton of times, but nobody ever answered. Bummer."

So, I knocked again, and still... dead silence

Cool. NOW I could leave.

But as I started walking away, the door suddenly went, CLUNK! and swung wide open, and as much as I'd LOVE to tell you that I reacted like a totally normal, NOT scared child... I can't.

The kid in the doorway laughed. The kid behind him laughed, too.

I recognized both of them.

I see them walking in the hallways between classes every single day. Well, every single day that's not the weekend.

So, every single SCHOOL day.

Sometimes I see them at lunch making sure nobody steals food.

Sometimes I see them before and after school to keep kids from running in the halls.

And this one time I saw them in the boy's locker room when some kid said his watch was stolen out of his backpack. There was a major investigation and everything. Crime scene analysis. Witness interviews. Locker shakedowns. The watch ended up being on the kid's wrist the whole time, BTW.

The two kids laughing at me were Parker Lee and Chad Schulte.

Hall Monitors.

Parker wiped the tears from his eyes, leaned over so we were face to face, and said...

EPISODE FIVE:
I AM... THE NOOB

SO...
I GUESS I'M A
HALL MONITOR
NOW...

112 VIEWS   137 FANS

Parker said he just got off the phone with Principal Hawkins who told him that I was going to be their newest recruit.

Hawkins' message was loud and clear.

By making me a Hall Monitor, Hawkins was saying, "Go find Pompom on your own," without actually saying the words, "Go find Pompom on your own."

NO, THAT'S NOT AT ALL
WHAT I'M SAYING. IN
FACT, ANIMAL CONTROL
IS ON THEIR WAY NOW
TO FIND POMPOM.

And let's not ignore the fact that an amazing opportunity had just landed in my YouTube channel's lap.

Yeah, Pompom ran away, which is bad. But if I found her, that would be good. And finding her on VIDEO would be even GOODER. Like, the GOODEST good!

Rescuing that chicken would be EPIC for my channel!

Besides, how hard could it be to find her? It's like a giant game of hide 'n seek where one of us is a near-genius and the other has a pea-sized brain.

Game on, Principal Hawkins.

Game. On.

Anyhow, Parker let me into the Hall Monitor office, which was more decked out than I expected it to be. And by "decked out," I mean there was an old sofa where Chad was playing Xbox on a 4K TV that was hanging on the wall.

HOW DO YOU GUYS EVEN HAVE A TV?

WE HAVE A BUDGET. WE TELL GLADUS WE NEED SOMETHING; SHE BUYS US THAT THING.

I TOLD HER THE XBOX AND TV WERE FOR SECURITY STUFF. HA! SUCKER!

Gladus works in the front office. She's the sweetest little, old lady in the whole world. Pretty sure she's around 90. Parker took advantage of her kind, elderly nature. The poor thing probably doesn't even know what an Xbox even is.

OKAY, **ONE** - I'M ONLY IN MY 40'S. AND **TWO** - THAT XBOX AND TV ARE COMIN' OUT **TONIGHT.**

Parker handed me an orange sash with a badge and told me to put it on. Gotta be honest here – it felt pretty good wearing that thing. Felt like I was suddenly somebody important at my school, like a Mr. Manager or something.

It was the feeling of power.

And I wanted more.

No whacking sticks. That was a little disappointing, but understandable.

To be honest, I wasn't sure if "whacking sticks" were a real thing or not. Like, in my head, I thought they were real, but in my heart, I knew they weren't.

Uh... anyways, moving right along...

After that, I figured I had to go through some training. Maybe watch an orientation video. Maybe some physical conditioning. Combat diving. Land warfare. Y'know – the same stuff Navy Seals go through.

But apparently not.

All it took for me to be a Hall Monitor was my autograph.

EPISODE SIX:
HALL MONITORS

HALL MONITORS IS FILMED ON LOCATION WITH THE KIDS OF LAW ENFORCEMENT.

ALL SUSPECTS ARE INNOCENT UNTIL PROVEN GUILTY IN THE COURT OF DETENTION.

122 VIEWS

134 FANS

My first patrol was between 5th and 6th period.

Parker said it was his LEAST favorite time of day because that's when students were at their peak levels of crazy.

AROUND NOW IS WHEN KIDS START GETTING ANTSY TO GET OUT OF SCHOOL.

36

All I wanted was to get out there and start lookin' for Pompom, but Parker didn't think I was ready to be on my own yet since I was still a noob.

He wanted to show me how it was done, which basically meant he wanted to show off.

I mean, wasn't the whole point of me joining the Hall Monitors to find Pompom?

NOOOOO, IT WAS TO TEACH DAVY **RESPONSIBILITY.**

Since Parker was basically the top banana, I figured I should listen to him. Hawkins wouldn't have been too happy if I butted heads with Parker on the first patrol I went out on.

That's fine. I could still keep an eye out for that chicken while I was on duty, so it wasn't that big of a deal.

Five minutes before 5th period ended, I packed up my books, hoisted my backpack over one shoulder, and slid out of my seat, swaggering toward the door like a BOSS.

My science teacher, Mr. Mitchell was like, "And just where do you think YOU'RE going, young man? I've still got you for another FIVE minutes!"

That's when I spun around, busted out my official Hall Monitor I.D. badge that I made during class, and said...

37

EVERYBODY in class LOST THEIR MINDS, cheering and chanting my name over and over. Mr. Mitchell even tried to calm them down but couldn't control the crowd. Confetti dropped from the ceiling, alarms started blaring, and ALL the girlies fell in love with me.

Parker wanted me to meet him in the front lobby, so that's where I went, scanning down every hallway I passed to see if Pompom was there.

She wasn't.

It had already been an hour since she ran off, so she could be anywhere. I mean, I'm not an expert in chicken things, so I really don't know how fast they can run. I want to say a hundred miles per hour, but... I don't know, I'm probably wrong. That sounds a little fast.

Pompom would've been in the Coast of Rico by then if she could run that fast.

When I got to the front lobby, Parker and Chad were standing around, wearing sunglasses and sipping on hot cups of black coffee.

Okay, let me just say... I don't wear sunglasses because they make me look like Mr. Potato Head, and I HATE coffee because it's basically dirt water, but I gotta admit... Parker and Chad looked SUPER cool.

Parker offered me a cup of Joe, and against my better judgement, I said yes. The first sip wasn't great. Neither was the second sip. Or the third. Or the fourth...

After that, Chad went off on his own patrol since he was a seasoned veteran, and Parker and I started making the rounds.

We walked up and down each hallway, waiting for the bell to ring. It wasn't the most exciting thing in the world, but it definitely beat sitting in a classroom. Parker called it "the quiet before the storm."

But as soon as the bell rang, I understood.

Annie, Chuck, and Fergus found me pretty quick, and guess what? They weren't even mad about the whole "getting them in a ton of trouble at lunch" thing!

Well, okay, CHUCK and FERGUS were fine, but Annie wanted a little something EXTRA for her forgiveness.

Parker told them that we had work to do, but I informed him we were kind of a package deal. Anywhere I go, they go.

*FYI - ENTOURAGE = BFFs.

Parker didn't argue. He just rolled his eyes and sighed. Good thing, too, because I couldn't imagine doing anything without my buds.

So, anyways, when you're a student at school, you don't really see all the crazy things that happen in the hallways. You're too busy trying to get to your next class with BARELY enough time to squeeze in a "Whuddup?" to your friends. Here's an example...

See? That was just two kids saying hi to each other, right?

WRONG.

What nobody noticed was the kid who was trapped in his locker behind them.

Parker went up to the locker to help the poor guy out who, apparently, had been stuck in there since the beginning of the school day.

Since Parker didn't have a master locker key, he had to text Chad to get it from the front office. Since there wasn't anything else we could do, we had to bail on the kid.

As we continued, I wanted to show Parker that I had what it took to be a Hall Monitor. That I didn't need a babysitter! That I was "big boy" enough to play by myself! That way, maybe he'd let me patrol on my own and I could go look for Pompom instead of doing all that other stuff. So, I busted out the megaphone that I snuck out of the Hall Monitor office and started shouting things like...

I sounded SUPES legit. Like, if you were there, you would've been like, "Wow, that kid sounds SUPES legit!" But no matter how loudly I barked out my orders, nobody really paid much attention to me.

And then we turned the corner and finally got face-to-face with some REAL action. A bunch'a students were gathered around a water fountain, lookin' all sorts of suspicious.

There was a possibility they were huddled around Pompom – a SMALL possibility, but still a possibility – so I propped my camera up on a selfie stick to get a high-angle shot for the heroic rescue scene.

Turns out, the crowd WASN'T for Pompom. It was for a kid named Greg, who was selling water balloons out of his backpack, which was so stupid-smart that I felt dumb for not having thought of it first.

He had one of those water balloon 100-packs where a hose fills all the balloons at the same time, then when a balloon is full, it falls off and ties itself like magic! Greg had even unhooked a hose from under the water fountain and was using that to fill the balloons!

And since he was the only kid at Wood selling water balloons, he charged whatever he wanted. They went for a buck a pop! By the time we got to him, he had already made SIXTY dollars! Auugh! IT WAS GENIUS, but... Parker didn't see it that way.

Since water balloons weigh more than you'd think, Greg didn't make it very far. He ran about halfway down the hall before he finally slipped, popping the rest of the balloons in his backpack and causing a HUMONGOUS mess.

And while Parker was texting Chad to bring him a mop, I suddenly heard the sound of something familiar...

I turned around, and yup. Pompom was clucking around at the end of the hallway. She was completely safe and unharmed! You have NO IDEA how much of a relief that was for me.

Me and my friends left Parker and slowly tip-toed toward the plump hen to try and sneak up on her. It worked for about a second, but then she did that thing that chickens do, snapping her head up and completely freezing in place.

I think I had triggered her "fight-or-flight" mode. Either she was about to go completely BONKERS and attack me or she was about to run again.

Honestly, I don't know which one I preferred.

Bonkers meant possibly catching Pompom, but also possibly getting my eyeball pecked out, which was NOT GOOD, obvi.

And running again meant losing her a second time, which was also NOT GOOD.

DECISIONS, DECISIONS.

I went with plan A, but only because I think scientists will learn how to grow new eyeballs for people in the future.

Actually, I didn't technically decide to do anything. My legs decided for me when Pompom took off like a rocket in the opposite direction.

GANGWAY! HALL MONITOR COMIN' THROUGH!

Kids freaked out as Pompom raced down the hall toward the side exit of the school. Pompom made the same move she did back in the cafeteria – she popped up, body slammed the door to open it, and went outside.

And right there, I didn't have a doubt in my mind – chickens know how to open doors.

At least, THAT chicken does.

I burst through the exit and ran outside, but I didn't get far. I got body-checked by a kid who was already out there.

It was like hitting a wall.

I stumbled back, falling on my butt, dizzy with pain. I thought I got walloped so hard that my ears had started ringing, but thankfully everybody else could hear it, too.

The boy who knocked me down stood over me with the skinniest jeans I've ever seen as a girl joined him by his side. Both of them were wearing the same style sash that I was, except theirs weren't orange. Theirs were black.

I didn't know who they were, but I knew why they were outside.

See, Hall Monitors take care of things INSIDE the school, but d'you know who takes care of things OUTSIDE?

Yup.

Student Patrol.

EPISODE SEVEN:
JURISDICTION FRICTION

APPARENTLY, HALL MONITORS AND STUDENT PATROL DON'T PLAY WELL TOGETHER...

▶ ❙❙   CC ✴ ▭ ❐

134 VIEWS   144 FANS

The only two kids on Student Patrol were a seventh grader named Elijah and an eighth grader named Evie, who also happened to be brother and sister.

Their job was to patrol the outside of Wood Intermediate between classes, which meant making sure nobody was ditching, helping kids cross the street, and getting everyone on the right buses after school.

When my head finally stopped spinning, I got back on my feet.

Parker had already followed me outside and was in a shouting match with Evie about who had jurisdiction over what and where.

Basically, Parker and I were out of bounds.

Things were a mess, but I didn't care. All I wanted to do was find Pompom!

53

Elijah said he never saw a chicken bust out of the school, but he had a weird half-smile when he said it. The kind of weird half-smile that people make when they're lying.

That's when Evie tucked her thumbs into her armpits and started bobbing her head at me while going, "Bok bok!"

Elijah quickly joined in, so the both of them were basically acting like big chickens. I think they were making fun of me and Parker, but I'm not 100% sure.

Then they kept "clucking" at us for, like, an AWKWARDLY long time. Like, WAY longer than they should have. It went past the point of being funny when Elijah started running out of breath, but still forced himself to "Bok!" like his life depended on it. His face was red and he was spittin' saliva out of his mouth and everything!

Finally, me and Parker just gave up and went back into the school. Besides, Pompom was already long gone by then, so it was no use trying to find her.

I still had five minutes left of my patrol with Parker, who had suddenly become very quiet.

He actually didn't say another word to me for the rest of our patrol.

EPISODE EIGHT:
VIEWER REQUEST: GAMERS PARADISE

127 VIEWS   145 FANS

One of you awesome Fans asked me to make my channel a GAMING channel, so this one's for you!

I've never tried making a gaming video, but I've WATCHED a bazillion of them, which pretty much makes me an expert at it.

There are some gamers who make BANK off their videos. Like, they're pulling in INSANE amounts of money just to sit around and play games all day.

It kinda makes me wonder why the heck I haven't done that yet! For real, if this video takes off, then I'm going gamer mode FULL-TIME after this and NEVER looking back.

It can't be that hard, can it? I mean, all I gotta do is point a camera at my face and talk while you watch me play Minecraft?

Um, YES, PLEASE.

So, after HOURS of research, I figured out what kind of gear I needed to make this video. It was kind of hard because there's TONS of different stuff out there.

I needed some game recording software, high-end microphones, HD cameras that are better than the janky one I've got, a bomb headset, a proper lighting rig, a professional editing studio... basically all the things I didn't have.

But I knew someone who did.

After school, I went over to Fergus' place, which didn't take long since he literally lives right next door to me. Fergus already had a whole gaming stream setup because he's been streaming gameplay on his YouTube channel since before my family even moved here.

His streams hardly get any views, but that might be because of the games he's plays. They're not exactly the hottest games on the market right now.

Since I was about to become the next greatest video game streamer, you know I had to do it right. During school, I had sent an email to Hacktronics, a local shop, and told them all about me, what I was gonna do, and where I was gonna be.

Then I gave them a chance to sponsor my channel, to which they gave me a big fat NO. I mean, I get it. I'm kind of a nobody right now so obviously Hacktronics is a little scared of throwing free stuff in my direction. But just for future reference, let me just tell you right now that when this video blows up, you guys at Hacktronics will WISH you had gotten on the Davy train before it left the station.

Anyways, since Hacktronics peaced out, I emailed a local drink factory and asked if THEY were interested.

They responded IMMEDIATELY because they were able to recognize greatness when they saw it. They told me they'd be happy to sponsor me!

I figured they'd send me an energy drink since that's what most gamer drink companies do, but that's not what they sent. Instead, they sent me a jar of something called "Gamer Gravy."

My friends thought drinking the gravy was a terrible idea. Not gonna lie – I wasn't pumped about it either, but what choice did I have? I was a video game streamer with an official sponsor! If I didn't make good on the deal, then I'd risk losing all my FUTURE sponsors, too!

So, I popped the lid off, squeezed my eyes shut, and chugged the whole jar. Well... I didn't really CHUG it. The gravy had some pretty big mushrooms I needed to chew first. It wasn't easy, but I horked the whole thing down like a champ.

Ugh.

The mushroom gravy wasn't sitting in my stomach very well, but I guess that makes sense. There was, in fact, an entire jar of gravy sloshing around in my tummy. And I wasn't really feeling the "energy" part yet. I really hoped it kicked in soon because I was starting to feel a nap coming on.

After that, I sat in Fergus' spot where he records his gaming stuff and asked him to launch Fortnite for me like he said he would when I asked him about it at school. FYI, like you don't already know, but Fortnite is one of the most popular games to stream, which is why I asked Fergus if he had it... well, APPARENTLY, he misheard me because instead of pulling up Fortnite... he led me into another room with an old school arcade machine and said...

HERE'S THE GAME YOU ASKED FOR!

FORK-KNIFE™!

THAT IS **NOT WHAT** I SAID.

FORK-KNIFE

FYI, because you actually DON'T know, Fork-Knife™ is some kind of old school arcade game where players do battle with the forces of hunger using nothing but kitchen utensils.

...yay.

Whatever. I still had Fans who were counting on me, a video to make, and a belly full of caffeinated mushroom gravy that was just starting to make my heart race.

It was go time.

But seriously, I could suddenly see my heartbeat in my eyes. Probably not a good thing.

I climbed onto a stool, hit the "Player 1" button, and got down to business.

Fork-Knife™ was not an easy game. In fact, it was SUPER hard. Like most vintage arcade games, it was designed to gobble up all your quarters with confusing levels, impossible bosses, and horrible controls. I'd try to explain more about the game, but it's tough since the whole thing didn't make much sense to begin with.

I kept dying over and over and over again because of the ridiculous picnic level where you gotta battle all these ants that want your food. Somebody must've programmed that game to cheat because every time I got close to beating it, a MILLION MORE ants swarmed the screen.

Pretty sure I played that level for hours.

Dutch was the only one who stuck by my side the whole way through. He told me that his dad used to take him to the arcade to play that exact game while he watched, and that the music was giving him some majorly nostalgic vibes.

At last — at very, very last — after the sun went down, and the Gamer Gravy had worn off, I was on the final boss of the game, which was a little old grandma who didn't want you to have seconds on dessert.

And finally, around midnight with an aching back, blisters on my fingies, and dried-up eyeballs, I beat the game. I raised my hands in victory... but that's when I started feeling lightheaded.

Part of it was from standing for seven hours straight. The other part was from the sugar crash from the Gamer Gravy. They should really put a warning on that stuff!

And before I zonked out, I gave Dutch my last words...

Someday, when the world sees that Fork-Knife™ arcade machine, they'll be like, "Here stood the greatest YouTuber of all time..." That arcade machine had officially become sacred and holy ground. Youtubers from all over the world

65

will flock to it just to be in the presence of awesomeness.

And I owe it all to Dutch, who promised to punch in my initials for the high score – the only proof I had of my great sacrifice.

Without my initials, it was all for nothing.

Dutch was the real hero that night.

After me, of course.

EPISODE NINE:
FOWL PLAY

TUESDAY...

DAY TWO OF THE CASE OF THE MISSING POMPOM.

▶ ‖

When I got to school, I was really hoping that the chicken had been found by Animal Control, but nope. Turns out, they hadn't even shown up yet! Hawkins told me that Animal Control won't LOOK for Pompom, so we were supposed to call them when we knew where she was so they could come and catch her.

But, like, if we KNEW where she was, we wouldn't need Animal Control.

Whatever, I guess.

Anyways, that meant Pompom was still missing.

Kids were talking about it in the hallways, too.

The whole way up to the Hall Monitor office, I was getting stares. And not the good kind, either, like when somebody's crushin' on you. No, these were the bad stares, like when you lose the school's favorite chicken named Pompom.

And when I got to Room FN-1027, I found out that the chicken wasn't the only thing that had gone missing. The Xbox and 4K TV were suddenly MIA.

Chad wasn't wrong.

I guess Gladus watches all my videos and might've been tipped off about the TV from my channel.

Parker was already mad at me cuz of what happened with the Student Patrol yesterday, but now Chad was mad because I lost his videogames.

Things were NOT going well, and it was only TUESDAY.

I wasn't too worried about it, though. I had brought something from home to help on my patrol. You know what every good police department has?

A K-9 unit.

That's right. I snuck Bo-Bo, my sister's dog, into the school using my backpack. I even made him an itsy-bitsy sash and everything.

HE'S BLIND, SO HE CAN'T REALLY DO ANYTHING, BUT HE'S MORE FOR LOOKS ANYWAYS.

Anyways, Parker HATED my idea. He immediately ratted me out to Principal Hawkins who ALSO hated my idea. Then Principal Hawkins called my dad at work and had him come pick Bo-bo up from school.

[sigh...]

After that, Chad took me out on patrol since Parker was too annoyed to even look at me. The first thing I did was put up giant "MISSING" posters of Pompom all over the schools along with a taping a bunch of smaller ones to milk cartons.

I was pretty sure that everybody already knew she was missing, but just in case there were some who hadn't gotten the memo yet - that poster was for them.

It was a pretty busy morning. First, I had to help an elderly gentleman find the library...

Then, Chad and I stopped a fight between a couple of eighth graders who were WAY bigger than us. Since our muscles were no match for them, we convinced them that beating each other with their fists wasn't as cool as beating each other on the chess board.

Honestly, we got lucky with that one. The only reason the fight ended was because of how confused the eighth graders were about the chess thing.

Then we went right from the chess game to a high-speed bike chase in the hallways because some wad thought it'd be hilarious to film himself flying through the school on his bike for his own YouTube channel.

Chad wanted to let the kid off easy with a warning, but how was he gonna learn his lesson without getting a consequence? I wrote him a ticket on the spot. Might not have been legit, but I think he got the point.

Right after that is when the big stuff happened. Chad and I were finishing up our morning patrol, making sure the school was clear of shenanigans, when we just happened to come across a dance battle in the hallways THE LIKES OF WHICH THIS EARTH HAS NEVER SEEN BEFORE!

Can you even believe it??

First of all, unicorns were long thought to be EXTINCT so that alone was the scientific discovery of the century, but the fact that they were in the middle of a DANCE BATTLE at Wood Intermediate?? That was absolutely MINDWRECKING.

The two unicorns danced like the universe depended on it because it probably did! I don't know enough about real-life unicorns to dispute that fact, so until then, we've gotta consider EVERY possibility, right?

It's just what good scientists do.

And to the haters who are gonna say it's fake, all I have to say to you is this... "Nuh-uh."

The battle only lasted a minute, but in unicorn time, that one minute might as well have been an eternity. Maybe it's good they weren't allowed to finish their fight since the full thing probably would've melted everybody eyeballs right out of their skulls.

That's when Chad kind of freaked and pulled the unicorn mask off Chuck and threw it on the ground.

Chad was pretty irked by the whole thing, but only because he thought it was a waste of time to film something like that. Parker obviously agreed with him.

I mean, it's not their fault that they don't get how YouTubing works.

Anyways, the bell rang.

School started.

And Pompom was still missing.

EPISODE TEN:
HALF PAST HEN

HALF A SCHOOL DAY LATER AND STILL... NO CHICKEN.

167 VIEWS   142 FANS

During lunch, instead of having me tag along for a patrol, Parker gave me some random duties to do by myself.

"Grunt work" is what he called it.

Shredding junk mail...

THIS ISN'T SO BAD...

SHRED!

Changing trashcan bags in the hallway...

And roping off an area outside of the cafeteria to redirect traffic because some kid barfed out there.

I was pretty down in the dumps about doing all those meaningless jobs, but it was around the puddle of stanktastic barf that I saw Pompom again from the corner of my eye.

She was back, poking her head out of the boy's bathroom!

That time, I didn't hesitate. I made a mad dash for the bathroom, diving onto my tummy and sliding across the floor like some kind of superhero right into the bathroom.

Pompom was in my hands. I did it! I finally caught her! And the best part was that she wasn't even spazzing out! I marched out of the bathroom, chicken cradled in my arms and announced...

She was perfectly still as I held her up for the world to see.

In fact, she was so perfectly still that it didn't even feel like she was breathing. I gave her a little squeeze. Her body was harder than I remember. Lighter too. And more... what's the word... hollow? That's when somebody shouted...

My face grew red as everybody laughed and pointed at me. I don't know if you've ever been in an embarrassing situation before, but time slows to a crawl when it happens. It felt like those kids were laughing at me for hours.

Even Miss Gymalski had joined in, but I don't think she really understood they were laughing AT me and not WITH me.

Parker marched up and slapped the fake chicken out of my hands. He was furious at me for making the Hall Monitors the laughingstock of the school.

I can't believe I fell for the ol' bogus chicken gag. The thing just looked so real. Whoever made it really put a lot of effort into it, using real feathers and everything, but who the heck would even do a thing like that?

About two seconds later, I got my answer...

Okay, I admit, they got me. I got punked by a harmless prank. That's fine. I mean, I'm a YouTuber, so I know what's up. I know EXACTLY how popular those kinds of videos are. And a fake chicken was a great idea, really it was...

But was the SECOND fake chicken outside the science lab a great idea?

Or the THIRD outside the gym?

Or the FOURTH? FIFTH? SIXTH fake chicken? I found more and more fake chickens all over the place between every class!

WERE THOSE GREAT IDEAS, TOO??

Evie and Elijah had made so many fake chickens that, by the end of the day, I had enough to start a fake farm. They were overflowing the Hall Monitor office. I was actually impressed that they were able to make so many paper mache chickens and find so many feathers so quickly.

But, while I wasn't mad, Parker and Chad were. But not at Evie and Elijah. They were mad at ME, like WHAT??

I know that Evie and Elijah were messing with ME, but it kind of felt like they were using me to humiliate Parker and Chad, too. What if this was their way of crushing the Hall Monitors so that Student Patrol would become the only authority in the school?

That sounds nuts, I know.

Evie and Elijah aren't actually evil villains with an elaborate plot to rule the school under their iron fists... right?

By the end of the school day, Pompom was still missing, but hey, if you ever need a fake chicken, I'm your guy!

EPISODE ELEVEN:
VIEWER'S REQUEST: PARKS AND REKT

IN THIS EPISODE, WE'LL BE TURNING CHUCK'S MOTEL INTO AN...

AMUSEMENT PARRRRRK!

152 VIEWS   141 FANS

But just so you know, that's WAY easier said than done.

Amusement parks have all kinds of different rides and food shacks and magic shows and animals and whatever...

All Chuck's motel has is a pool.

And even THAT'S kind of crummy.

I MEAN, HE'S RIGHT, BUT COME ON!

To be honest, I didn't think we'd get very far with this project. I kinda figured Chuck's dad would squash it from the start, but he didn't.

In fact... he was INTO it.

After we got permission, we needed to get funding. Building rides costs money! Money that me and my peeps didn't have. But Chuck's dad was totally cool with that, too!

Chuck's parents and my parents went on a double date together, which gave us PLENTY of time to make a carnival that would BLOW THEIR MINDS by the time they got back.

Since Annie's the artist of our group, she drew up a ton of plans for different rides. Most of them were a little TOO cray-cray, like the giant slingshot that launched you across the parking lot, but some were pretty dope, like the slide that went from the roof of the motel into the pool. She called it the "You Might Die Slide."

OKAY, BUT THE SLIDE DOESN'T REACH THE POOL!

THAT'S WHY THE SIDEWALK IS WET! WHEN YOU HIT THE CEMENT, YOU'LL SLIDE THE REST OF THE WAY INTO THE POOL!

*DO NOT TRY THIS AT HOME. DUH.

Another great idea that was just as easy to pull off was the ride she called the "Spin Master," which was where you try to not fall off an office chair with a leaf blower pointed at it, cranked to the highest setting. Don't worry. My sister tested it out, and it's totally safe.

THIS IS MORE FUN FOR HER THAN IT IS FOR ME.

*DO NOT TRY THIS AT HOME. DUH.

Then there was my personal favorite, the "Swingy Ding," which was just a bunch of swings tied to a ceiling fan.

*DO NOT TRY THIS AT HOME. DUH.

The only thing left before opening the gates was naming the amusement park. Annie, Chuck, and Fergus wanted to go with "Way Cool Adventure Park," but I wanted to go with something a little classier – The Land of Davy.

Since there were two names, we took a vote.

Obviously, I lost, but only because real genius almost never gets the street-cred it deserves.

Anyways, Way Cool Adventure Park opened, and the crowd poured in. And by "crowd," I mean "nobody."

Not a single person showed up, and in case you don't know, the most important part of running a business is having customers!

I mean, I get it - the park was a last-minute idea, but I thought at least a FEW people would stop by. I even sent emails out to all my Fans about it! And not just one email, but like, a hundred.

That way they'd know it was important!

Annie, Chuck, and Fergus were pretty bummed about the failure, and to be honest, I was, too. But after the last couple days I had, I wasn't about to just throw in the towel. Nope. I had failed enough.

So, I rolled up my sleeves, looked up some businesses, and made one of the most important phone calls of my life...

The cool thing about Rent-A-Carnival was that they didn't need to build rides from scratch. It was a business that had all their rides already built, just sitting on semi-trucks and waiting to be delivered. They guaranteed a fully functional carnival in less than an hour or your money back.

And yes, I know an amusement park and a carnival are two different things. But... are they really?

Anyways, the crew from Rent-A-Carnival showed up about twenty minutes later, ready to get to work. Their website said they had three different sizes to choose from.

Big. Bigger. And Biggest.

Normally, I try to save money whenever I can, but since I wasn't using MY money, I went with their Biggest option.

The Rent-A-Carnival boss said they only needed an hour, so me and my friends went inside to play some Super Smash Bros. while we waited.

NOAH, YOU CAN'T BE KIRBY THIS TIME! YOU'RE TOO STRONG WITH KIRBY!

YEAH, YOU GOTTA BE PICHU!

BUT PICHU'S THE **WORST!**

No offense, Pichu, but it's true.

Get some better moves and we'll talk.

Finally, there was a knock at the door. The hour breezed by, and the carnival was all set up and ready to go.

I'm gonna go ahead and say... I didn't expect much from a

business called Rent-A-Carnival. I thought maybe they'd bring some kiddie rides like a mini-carrousel with cute, little horses.

Maybe one of those quarter rides like they have at the mall with spaceships and monster trucks or whatever.

At the MOST, I thought they'd bring a little train to drive around the parking lot.

But nope.

I was totally wrong about ALL of that.

They literally brought an entire carnival with them.

And guess what? I didn't need to worry about inviting anybody because people started strolling in on their own!

Random people driving by saw all the lights and rides and pulled into the El Rancho parking lot to see what it was all about! Then they STAYED because of how COOL it was!

People texted their friends who texted their friends who texted their friends who texted their friends and within thirty minutes, the place was PACKED. People came from all over, even those familiar kids from that other thing!

It was absolutely bonkers in the best way possible.

Totally unplanned. Totally unexpected. And totally awesome.

But that's when our parents got back. More important, that's when Chuck's DAD got back.

TA-DAAA...

My parents and Chuck's parents were pretty shocked, eyes wide with jaws dropped and all that stuff.

For the longest time, they just stood there, staring.

For the longest time... just staring.

No words. No movement. No blinking.

Just silence that a lot of people call "awkward."

Chuck watched his dad's face, waiting for him to say something, anything.

Actually, Chuck's mom and my parents had started watching his face, too. So were me, Annie, and Fergus. We ALL watched Chuck's dad's face for any kinds of signs of anger.

Finally, he folded his arms, took a deep breath, and looked at Chuck.

Then, he said...

Chuck's dad wasn't even mad about how much the Rent-A-Carnival cost – he was just pumped that the party was at the El Rancho because it reminded him of the "good ol' days," when the motel first opened and they had guests every single night.

We spent the rest of the night riding rides, eating junk food, and having an absolute blast.

Overall, it was a pretty good end to a pretty horrible day.

EPISODE TWELVE:
THE FLEETING FOWL

SO, IT'S WEDNESDAY, AND STILL...

NO. STINKIN'. CHICKEN.

First thing Wednesday morning, I started looking for Pompom with Annie and Chuck instead of with Parker and Chad. I'm pretty sure they had given up on the idea of finding her, but I definitely hadn't.

WE DIDN'T GIVE UP ON IT! WE'VE JUST GOT MORE IMPORTANT THINGS TO DO!

YEAH! THESE HALLS AREN'T GONNA MONITOR THEMSELVES!

Pompom was still out there somewhere, I just knew it, and I was determined to find her no matter how long it took.

On Tuesday, I had put up a bunch of "MISSING" posters for her, but then I was like, "What good is a 'MISSING' poster if people didn't know who to call if they found Pompom?"

So, I put up a bunch of NEW posters, but this time I added little tear-away slips on the bottom with a phone number to call if somebody saw something, even if it was just a CLUE and not the actual chicken.

But since I don't have my own cell phone, I put down the next best number I could think of, which was Principal Hawkins' number. Who better to call than the man in charge? At least, that's what I THOUGHT.

Turns out, Hawkins wasn't too happy with the idea.

At first, I was like, "Why doesn't he want kids calling him??"

But then, after he let me hear his voicemail, I was like, "Oh, okay, that's why..."

After me and my friends took down all the new posters, I decided to try and set up a couple traps for Pompom.

Not traps that would hurt her, because that would defeat the purpose of rescuing her, right? No, they were traps to catch her safely, duh.

The first trap we set was the classic "bait-under-a-box" trap, famously used by every cartoon since the beginning of time, but there might've been a disagreement about what kind of bait to use.

We finally agreed on using popcorn as bait since none of us really knew what we were doing. Annie made a path out of the little popped corn that led all the way down the hallway. Then the four of us hid around the corner and waited for the trap to fall.

We didn't have to wait long. Like, thirty seconds later, the trap was triggered. And it worked perfectly, except for one tiny detail... it wasn't Pompom that we caught.

It was Aksel, the weirdo from Survival Club.

Annie and Chuck bailed after that because they needed to get stuff from their lockers before school started, so I recruited Fergus and Dutch for trap #2, which was a little more complicated than the first one.

See, I hung a net over the middle of the hallway that would come down on Pompom if she ever walked under it. You're probably wondering how I built a trap that was sophisticated enough to know the difference between a chicken and a human.

That's where Fergus and Dutch came in.

The plan was simple – Dutch would hold the rope that released the net that Fergus would tell him to let go of when Pompom appeared to eat the popcorn that I'd use as bait again.

BECAUSE THAT WORKED SO WELL THE **FIRST** TIME.

It was a pretty great idea, but with one humongous problem... I realized that if Pompom SAW us then she'd know that something was up and run away all scared.

To fix that, I made the three of us a bunch of duck hunt styled camouflage suits (clothes that look like grass) along with a fake bush I borrowed from the Theatre Department. I got the idea after seeing Aksel in his Survival Club outfit.

Anyways, I threw a bunch of popcorn down on the floor and me, Fergus, and Dutch hid behind the bush, waiting for Pompom to take the bait.

Just waiting... and waiting... and more waiting...

And then the same thing happened to me that happens every time I need to hide. I suddenly had to pee. Like, BAD.

I'm the WORST at hide 'n seek because of my bladder! I NEVER have to go as badly as I do when I'm trying to hide! I did my best to hold it in for as long as possible, but it was no use. I only lasted about a minute.

I burst out of the bushes and ran to the boy's bathroom as fast as I could. And when I was done, I was washing my hands, all alone in there, when I suddenly heard a familiar sound again...

It came from one of the stalls.

I slowly walked over as the quiet little "boks" kept coming. My skin tingled as my heart raced. Either there was a runaway chicken sitting on the toilet or this bathroom had the weirdest sounding water leak ever.

When I got the stall door, I gently pushed it open.

And weirdly enough... Pompom WAS there.

Okay, don't freak out.

No sudden movements.

Be cool. You got this.

Just remain calm while picking Pompom up. She wasn't scared. Her feathers weren't ruffled. She was just chillin' in the boy's bathroom for some reason – not the most luxurious place to relax, but whatever, who am I to judge? The only important thing was that I found her.

Now, all I needed was to catch her.

My fingers grazed her feathers. She fluttered a bit but didn't run.

It was happening.

I was doing it.

In about ten seconds, I was gonna bust outta that bathroom with a live chicken in my hands and an entire school CHEERING for me, forgiving me for all the bad things I'd ever done.

It's a bizarre feeling – knowing you're about to reach hero status. So many thoughts raced through my brainium in that moment, like who should I hug first?

What should my first words be?

Should I accept a sponsorship deal with Xbox or hold out for PlayStation?

And most importantly – should I dedicate my heroic deeds to Emma Walsh, the prettiest girl in the whole wide world?

I had no doubt that Pompom's rescue would be covered in the yearbook like, "Davy Spencer: Hero to All Chickens." In fact, I should probably start thinking about what kind of haircut to get for my school picture on Friday.

Would a mohawk be an appropriate or should I go with something a little more classy, like a mullet?

Pompom let me wrap my fingers under her. She was cradled in my hands. It was WAY easier than I thought! That is, until Parker barged into the bathroom like a crazy person.

Needless to say, Pompom lost her chill. I tried gripping her tighter, but that didn't work because have you ever tried holding a freaked-out chicken?

It's not easy. Or fun.

Pompom hit the ground running.

Parker dove after her, but she dodged him like a ninja-chicken, dashing through his legs and out the door.

The screams of the students out there still haunt my nightmares to this day.

Parker and I ran out of the bathroom. He pointed a hard finger and said, "There she is! Get her!"

Pompom stopped to look at us with her cold, beady eyes like she was egging us on.

...

Get it?

EGGING?

Cuz she's a chicken?

Yeah, no, back to the story...

Pompom turned on her chicken heel and blitzed through all the kids standing in her way. They split apart like the Red Sea did when Moses did that thing with his hands.

She was headed right towards the trap I'd set with Dutch and Fergus.

Booyah.

I shouted at the two of them, but they were already on top of it. Fergus had his hand up, ready to tell Dutch to drop the net when Pompom was over the target.

I sprinted harder to get to them so I could scoop Pompom up after she got caught. Parker followed close behind me.

And when Pompom scurried past Dutch, Fergus dropped his hand, and the net was cast.

The plan worked perfectly.

Except the "perfectly" part.

No, Pompom was WAY too fast, like lightning fast. By the time the net hit the ground, she was already past it, and instead of catching the chicken...

I caught myself. And Parker.

EPISODE THIRTEEN:
THE LUNCH BUNCH

FYI - STILL NO BIRD. BUT AS PUNISHMENT FOR EMBARRASSING THE HALL MONITORS AGAIN, I GOT ASSIGNED TO LUNCH DUTY...

SO, GO ME...

146 VIEWS   132 FANS

Lunch duty is such a drag because the crowd outside the cafeteria is a ginormous mess of hangry kids waiting to eat.

Like, NOBODY'S ever in a good mood out there.

And the only thing that seemed to make them happy was picking on the Hall Monitor, AKA... me.

Listen, I totally understand how the internet works. I know that when someone becomes a famous influencer, especially on YouTube, they're gonna get haters.

It's just part of the gig, right?

But it's pretty lame when the haters come BEFORE the fame. I mean, I know it's my own fault. One – everybody was still upset that I lost Pompom. And two – I've been a pretty easy mark for the last couple days because of my

Hall Monitor videos. But honestly, I was only trying to help.

Anyways, I was directing traffic outside the cafeteria when Evie and Elijah showed up.

Like I wasn't in a bad mood already, right?

I don't even know what they were doing inside the school. Those two were Student Patrol! Their job was OUTSIDE, doing whatever they were supposed to be doing, I don't know, parking cars or something?

But they seemed to be perfectly happy hanging around and giving me a hard time. Some of their burns didn't make any sense, but some were actually pretty good. Funny, even. I couldn't help but crack up at a couple of them.

And then, in the middle of their dis-fest, I spotted a white blur zip across the floor.

Evie spun around, pointing. Then she shouted, "IT'S POMPOM! SOMEBODY GRAB THAT BIRD!"

Elijah nudged me with his elbow. "You better get her, dude, before she runs away again!"

I don't know why they were helping, but I didn't care – the universe was giving me a second chance (more like fourth or fifth chance) at catching that chicken, and I wasn't about to waste it! I gave it everything I had, running at full tilt.

Pompom weaved through the crowd, moving a little differently than before. I really hoped she wasn't hurt and limping or anything because there was def something wrong with her.

I smashed through clusters of students like they were the bowling pins, and I was the bowling ball. Books and papers and kids came raining down around me as I pursued that chicken on foot.

Then Pompom bolted into the school kitchen and started bounding around the back where the refrigerators were. Lunch ladies and gentlemen stumbled back with trays of food in their hands. That's when I blasted through the kitchen doors so fast that I couldn't stop myself...

I don't think I need to tell you what happened next...

BECAUSE OBVIOUSLY

Yeah, it was pretty bad.

Food was everywhere. I think tables were destroyed, but I'm not too sure. Everything just happened so fast. Kitchen staff were scolding me. Parker and Chad were in the doorway, shaking their heads. And Evie and Elijah were behind them, laughing their brains out, not sure why, but again, whatever... at least I had Pompom.

I held her tight enough that she couldn't squirm out of my hands, but it wasn't necessary. She seemed pretty happy to be there with me.

In fact, she was so happy that she barked and started licking my face...

Okay, wait... I'm not a bird doctor or anything, but I'm pretty sure chickens don't bark.

Do chickens lick, though? Do they even have tongues? Well, I don't know about the licking part, but I'm 100% positive that they DON'T BARK.

AH, MAN...

Yeah, the chicken in my hands was less of a chicken and more of a dog DRESSED as a chicken.

Evie and Elijah GUFFAWED (which means they were laughing like DONKEYS) behind Parker and Chad.

So... that's why Evie and Elijah were helping me earlier... It was THEIR dog that they had brought from home, and it was just another one of their dumb pranks.

Ugh... punked again.

EPISODE FOURTEEN:
VIEWER REQUEST: ME VS DUTCH

IT'S WEDNESDAY NIGHT, AND POMPOM HAS BEEN GONE FOR THREE WHOLE DAYS NOW...

132 VIEWS   142 FANS

I'm not giving up, but... I just needed something to take my mind off it, y'know? Something to distract me from the constantly pounding thoughts in my head that Pompom was gonna get hurt, and there was no one else to blame but me.

Physical activity helps with that, and what better physical activity than a 1v1 Smackdown in my backyard between me and Dutch?

It's a video that one of my Fans asked for, and remember, if you have an idea for one of my videos, just leave it in the comments! Or a review... or email... or whatever...

Anyways, Dutch wasn't super into the idea of smacking down because he said he was trying to be a better kid since he started hanging out with us. I understood that, but I explained that it wasn't gonna be a FIGHT with our fists. Heck no, I'd lose THAT in a heartbeat since I'm only ten and he's fourteen with MONSTER-sized hands.

Nope, our fight was gonna be with pillows. Or, as the ancient Olympians called it, a PILLOW FIGHT.

That way, Dutch could hit me as hard as he wanted to and I wouldn't feel a thing!

At least, that's what I THOUGHT would happen. The second our match started, he slammed me with a pillow so hard that it felt like I got hit by a truck.

*STARS ADDED DIGITALLY.

I got up for round 2, hoping to get a couple good swings in before getting whacked again, but for as big as that kid is, he's pretty quick on his toes.

He dodged my pillow attacks all smooth and gracefully like some kind of freaking gazelle or something. Seriously! I couldn't hit him no matter how hard I tried!

Dutch wound up another swing and gave me a wallop that sent me halfway across my yard.

Then what happened next is kind of a blur...

I remember hopping back to my feet for round 3 and totally DEMOLISHING Dutch with a whirlwind of Kung Fu pillow strikes, but all that must've been just in my head because my friends told me later that I never got up after Dutch's second shot.

EPISODE FIFTEEN:
JUICE OF THE TUNA

HEY, JUST SO YOU KNOW... I REALLY HATE TUNA JUICE.

LIKE, A LOT.

142 VIEWS

150 FANS

On Thursday, instead of going on patrol, Parker gave me a bunch of work to do in the Hall Monitor office instead. More "grunt work," but this time it was behind closed doors.

I mean, I get it. Because of me, the Hall Monitors had lost a lot of respect from the Student Patrol.

WELL, THAT'S JUST **NOT** TRUE.

YEAH, WE **NEVER** RESPECTED THE HALL MONITORS.

Anyways, for the first half of the day, I did everything Parker asked me to. Emptied the trash. Filed some papers. Vacuumed the carpet. Dusted some dusty stuff. He even had me unstaple a bunch of papers and then REstaple them back together.

Before school. Between classes. During lunch.

It was boring. Pointless. A complete waste of time. It was like watching paint dry.

Have you ever done that? Watch paint dry?

No?

You know why?

BECAUSE IT'S BORING.

So, yeah, I did that pretty much until noon. And when the lunch bell finally rang, I busted out of that office and headed to cafeteria to get my grub on.

But I didn't get far before seeing Pompom AGAIN. She was just bobbling around in the middle of one of the hallways, all by herself, not a care in the world.

Obviously, it WASN'T the real Pompom. It was another one of Evie and Elijah's fake chickens.

They were trying to prank me again.

Too bad I was smarter than that.

I walked toward the little toy and rolled my eyes. It's like they didn't even TRY to make this one look real. CLEARLY, it was a balloon filled with water that they drew eyes and a beak on. They did such a terrible job with the decoy that it was almost INSULTING.

Did they really think I was THAT dumb? That I couldn't tell the difference between a living chicken and a water balloon?

Parker and Chad turned the corner and stopped when they saw me reach for the balloon.

I don't know what the big deal was. I've held water balloons before – I know how to keep them from popping. I picked it up gently and felt all the water slosh around inside.

I'll admit, it wasn't the lamest prank in the world. Getting drenched by a water balloon is pretty harmless if you think about it. Annoying maybe, but harmless.

Parker and Chad started running toward me at full speed, shouting at me to put the balloon down like it was dangerous or something.

I didn't know why they were so worked up, that is, until I turned my head and saw Evie and Elijah behind me. Elijah was clapping with joy as Evie launched a pencil toward me like a throwing knife.

All I could do was watch the pencil spin through the air as Parker and Chad both dove at it, trying to slap the pencil out of the way, but they both missed, and the yellow pencil stuck the chicken balloon I was holding.

The thing EXPLODED with the force of a thousand supernovas, soaking me, Parker, and Chad with everything inside it.

The three of us stood there, shocked and dripping wet.

Oh, and FYI, we found out that the balloon WASN'T filled with water.

It was filled with...

You know the juice that's inside tuna cans that you have to drain before eating? It's LITERALLY stinky fish water.

Our clothes were SOAKED in it.

Evie and Elijah were rolling on the floor, laughing their butts off about the whole thing as students began to cluster around us.

They pointed. Made ugly faces. Pinched their noses. Some even took out their cell phones and texted pics of us to their friends.

Parker was FURIOUS, madder than he'd been about ANYTHING that week. He shouted a whole lotta ugly things at me. Things I probably shouldn't repeat if I wanna keep my YouTube channel "kid friendly."

Being covered in tuna juice was already humiliating enough, but Parker chewing me out in front of everybody just made it worse.

All that, PLUS the fact that Pompom was still missing made this week very close to being the worst one of my life.

After Parker was finished, he only said one more thing...

The bell rang, and I was left standing by myself in the hallway, tuna juice drying on my clothes and getting all crusty as kids returned to their classes.

I wasn't really sure why I didn't clean myself up right away.

Maybe I was in shock, I don't know.

But here's one thing I DID know... it was no longer VERY CLOSE to being the worst week of my life.

It had officially BECOME the worst week of my life.

EPISODE SIXTEEN:
AFTER SCHOOL BLUES

When I got home, I got a call from Emma because she thought I could use some cheering up. She asked if I wanted to hang out at the mall with her.

Uh, yes, please. Like, duh.

So, I rode my bike (BTW – I got a new bike since season 2) to meet her.

I didn't invite Annie, Chuck, Fergus, or Dutch... but I'm pretty sure they were there, too. I mean, I never SAW them, but I could feel their presence...

Emma and I didn't even do anything special. No shopping or nothin'. We just got a couple milkshakes and sat in the food court the whole time. She got strawberry while I went with something a little more... extravagant.

I got peanut butter pretzel bark with Oreo and fudge, topped with Nutella and whipped cream with a dusting of hot chocolate powder. Plus four cherries, half a banana, a fried Twinkie, and sliced strawberries with strawberry syrup lightly drizzled over all of it. Sprinkles over all that. Caramel syrup over that. Mini-chocolate chips over that. Waffle cone crumbles over that. Another layer of fudge. And then one last cherry on top.

What? Sometimes I eat my feelings. Sue me.

Hanging out was nice, and definitely the distraction I needed after a long week of awfulness.

I didn't even realize how down I was until we started talking about it. I mean, I knew I was bummed out, but not THAT bummed out. I wondered how she could even tell.

I mean, I'm ME, and I couldn't even tell.

Anyways, me and Emma showed each other a bunch of different YouTube videos that we loved. Emma liked watching gamers game. She watches that kind of stuff for hours without ever getting tired of it – even for games she'd never played before, like Fork-Knife™.

Then I showed her some of my favorites, mostly the ones where CRAZY RICH YouTubers are, like, "I bought over one million of SOMETHING and now we're gonna do something CRAZY with them!"

Those are the best.

The two of us hung around the food court a little while longer, laughing and joking before we had to leave. I think I could've stayed there all night if I were allowed to. Watching funny videos is such a great way to unwind.

Emma gave me a big hug goodbye and told me to never give up because my videos made her happy. Even the ones I thought were lame. She said those were her favorites because they showed the real me or something.

After that, I grabbed my bike from the rack outside and rode home.

Pretty sure I had a smile on my face the whole time, too.

At least, until I rolled up to my driveway. That's when I saw Evie, Elijah, Parker and Chad standing outside my house, throwing eggs at it. Parker and Chad were even wearing Student Patrol sashes! They had joined the dark side!

I couldn't believe my eyes! There were, like, TWENTY empty egg cartons on the ground! And when they saw me, they DIDN'T stop! They didn't even care that I was watching them egg my house!

It was like they WANTED me to see!

Finally, my mom peeked out the front window and went berserk when she saw what was happening. She had that angry look on her face – the kind I see in my nightmare sometimes. She was about to unleash the MONSTER on those kids out there. It was gonna be a scolding so harsh

128

that kids around the world would shudder without knowing why.

My mom pulled open the door, face red with rage, finger pointed stiffly at those kids, when suddenly...

Evie, Elijah, Parker, and Chad bolted immediately when that happened. Good thing, too, because if they had still been around when my mom wiped the raw egg out of her eyes, then you don't even wanna KNOW what would've happened.

I thought my parents were gonna be mad at ME because of our egg-covered house, but they weren't.

They were actually pretty cool about it.

Not about our house getting egged.

No, they were NOT cool about that. They just weren't mad that it was MY fault.

BUT IT'S **NOT DAVY'S FAULT! I WISH** HE WOULD STOP SAYING THAT!

Me and my parents spent the rest of the night cleaning up the mess that the Student Patrol had made. My dad hosed the side of the house while me and my mom scooped raw egg out of the places the water couldn't spray.

Honestly, it wasn't hard work, and my parents were doing their best to make me smile.

But no matter how hard they tried, it didn't really work.

It's not easy to smile when you know that everybody hates you.

EPISODE SEVENTEEN:
THE LAST HALL MONITOR

I mean, she's not dead. Not that I know of.

At least... I REALLY hoped she wasn't dead.

Anyways, when I got to school on Friday morning, I got some pretty grim looks from the other students.

I get it. I messed up. Kids were gonna be mad for a while.

Actually, LONGER than a while probably. It was possible that this whole thing would follow me all the way through high school. Maybe even college.

Man, I bet my own KIDS will have to deal with it someday, like, "Oh, Davy Spencer is your DAD? Did you know that HE HATES CHICKENS SO BAD THAT HE SETS 'EM FREE INTO THE WILD SO THEY HAVE NO CHANCE OF SURVIVAL AND ALSO HIS YOUTUBE CHANNEL IS THE WORST ONE ON THE INTERNET??? HE PROBABLY HATES PUPPIES, TOO!"

That's an exaggeration, but I bet it's not far from the truth.

Um, back to the story...

So, I tried finding my friends – Annie, Chuck, Fergus... even Dutch, but they weren't around anywhere. Maybe they were avoiding me, I don't know, maybe not. But the way everything else was going in my life, I wouldn't be surprised.

I was so miserably alone, trudging through that crowd, up the stairs to the second floor, to the Hall Monitor office.

AN ACCURATE DEPICTION OF MY FEELINGS FOR BEING MISERABLY ALONE...
ALSO... THAT DUCK IS BACK.

I'VE NAMED HIM SIR QUACKINGHAM PALACE.

Technically, it was just MY office now since I was the ONLY Hall Monitor left after Parker and Chad rage quit yesterday. That fact ALSO technically made me the Hall Monitor CAPTAIN, but what good is being a captain when nobody's on your team?

I didn't want to go on patrol by myself. Heck, I didn't even want to be a Hall Monitor let alone the ONLY Hall Monitor!

But what choice did I have? I couldn't quit like Parker and Chad because Principal Hawkins MADE me be a Hall Monitor as my punishment for losing Pompom.

Oh well. The only thing pushing me forward was the fact that it was Friday, and there were only seven more hours until school let out.

I could last that long.

Then I'd just plant myself on the basement couch with a gallon of chocolate milk, a whole loaf of buttered toast, and play Minecraft all weekend to reset my emotions for a fresh start next week.

When I got to the Hall Monitor Office door, it was cracked open an inch and the lights were on. That's when I heard voices inside, but they WEREN'T Parker's or Chad's.

Great.

Probably just some randos messing up the place as a prank. I bet they were in there knocking everything over and tagging the walls with spray paint or something.

My blood started to boil just thinking about it.

Sure, I was the most bummed out I'd ever been in my life, but that didn't mean that kids could walk all over me!

All my feelings came bubbling up. Sweat beaded up on my nose. My knees started shaking. My teeth started grinding.

Then I took a deep breath, kicked the door wide open, and wanted to shout some kind of super awesome one-liner like, "I hope you're ready for class, cuz you're all about to get SCHOOLED by me!"

But my brain always farts when I'm on the spot, so instead, I shouted...

The kids in the room weren't just random students. It was Annie, Chuck, Fergus, and Dutch. No wonder why I couldn't find them earlier.

But... WHY were they in my office?

I'm not gonna lie...

I totes broke down.

I couldn't help it! I didn't even know I had an "ugly cry" inside of me waiting to come out! I even tried to stop, but when I asked them WHY they wanted to help me, Fergus' answer just made me cry HARDER.

"Because THAT'S what FRIENDS do," he said.

I told them how I wished I could just quit like Parker and Chad, but Annie gave me some pretty wise advice...

I wiped my nose and sniffled. Annie was right. Pompom was

gone, and nothing I did could bring her back. But that didn't mean I should just give up on everything else. And yeah, that was my own interpretation of Annie's advice.

It's not WHAT she said; it's HOW she said it.

When I finally got ahold of myself, I immediately deputized my friends and gave them their sashes because the hallways were lawless without monitors.

Then we all headed out to the hallway to do our duties before school started. I was suddenly pumped about the job. Funny how that works, right? When something lame suddenly becomes fun just because all your best friends are doing it with you?

The morning was filled with the glorious monitoring of the hallways so amazeballs that history books will be filled with the grandiose tales of our adventures.

Fergus and Dutch totally crushed it together. They were the last two kids on Earth I'd expect to ever buddy up, but they went together like salt and pepper! Fergus even took the megaphone from the Hall Monitor office to make his voice more commanding.

And I gotta say that Dutch really pulled a 180 on all of us. At the beginning of the year, he was a total jerktastic bully, but now he was the guy who BUSTED bullies.

But I have to admit, the power might've gone to Fergus and Dutch's heads a little. Pretty soon, they weren't just busting on bad guys. They were busting on anybody who broke the rules, no matter who they were!

Then there was Annie... she found out the hard way that Greg was still messing around with water balloons, but he wasn't selling them this time. He was launching them.

On a routine investigation of a water main break in the west hall, Annie discovered Greg's secret plan to drench ALL the kids at Wood Intermediate.

Greg had built something he called a Doomsday Slingshot using nothing more than bungie cords, some wood, and a big bowl. Pretty simple stuff, but here's the kicker – instead of using tiny-sized water balloons, he was using NORMAL-sized balloons filled with water.

The kinds of balloons people blow up for birthday parties.

Yeah, those things can hold, like, a whole GALLON of water. So, when Annie got there, Greg had just finished filling a couple of them and was ready to launch the first one...

And then he did it.

Annie was soaked to the BONE. And you know that little voice inside your head that keeps you from doing crazy things. The one that's like, "This is a bad idea. You shouldn't do it."

Yeah, that voice in Annie's head was gone.

She totally snapped.

STOP RUNNING, GREG! I JUST WANNA GIVE YOU A HUG! FOR REAL!

For the record, Annie didn't hurt him.

She just gave him a taste of his own medicine.

Moving right along to Chuck... who busted an ENTIRE black-market operation in the east hall!

FYI – a black-market is any place that sells stuff that SHOULDN'T be selling stuff.

See, there's one dark hallway that 99% of people at Wood Intermediate don't go down because there's only one room there – the orchestra room. It's big enough that it kind of needs its own section of the school.

Well, in that section of the school, there are lockers that have been pretty much forgotten about by teachers. And apparently, in a place where locker inspections didn't exist, an entire convenient store rose up.

So, this is how it all went down...

Chuck noticed a bunch of kids coming out of the east hall with handfuls of snacks, and since Chuck is a big fan of snacks, he thought it was weird...

After a little stakeout, he discovered a student named Amos selling snacks right out of his locker. Like, his locker was PACKED with all kinds of different chips.

But it didn't end there. EVERY single locker in that hallway was FILLED with different merch! Chips. Soda. Candy. Pens. Pencils. Pokemon cards. Nintendo games. Small Lego sets. Comic books. There was even FRESH FRUIT. It was like Amos had opened his own Super Target in the east hall!

It's crazy - Amos brought a backpack full of fun stuff every single day to fill those lockers with - lockers that he paid students to rent (not with money, but with snacks), which is how he owned ALL of them down there.

Chuck shut it all down when he found out about it. Amos went directly to detention, and the students in the east hall got their lockers back.

And finally, there was me.

My patrol wasn't as exciting as Annie, Chuck, Fergus, or Dutch's. In fact, nothing happened on my patrol that's even worth talking about...

Seriously, it was boring...

Nothing to call home about...

Except for...

THE REAL POMPOM SHOWING UP AGAIN!

I was walking past the cafeteria when I heard all the kids in there FREAKING out, like, completely losing their minds. The doors bashed opened and students came POURING out, screaming about a loose chicken.

I ran up to the doors to look inside, and heck yes, it was Pompom! When everybody was out of the cafeteria, I slammed the doors shut to trap the chicken inside. Hopefully Animal Control could get there and catch her now that we knew where she was!

Annie, Chuck, Fergus, and Dutch came running up behind me.

So did Parker, Chad, Evie, and Elijah.

My buddies all wanted to know what my plan was, but the only thing I could think of was to wait for Animal Control.

Evie and her squad started making fun of me because of course they did, talkin' about how I was gonna fail all over again with the whole school watching.

Gonna be honest here... I don't really like Student Patrol.

Pompom was going ABSOLUTELY BONKERS in the cafeteria, squawking and smashing against the doors like some kinda monster. I don't know what got into her, but she was MAD.

I looked at my friends like, "What do we do?" but they were looking at me the same way.

Then Fergus pulled out his megaphone again...

That didn't work.

Obviously.

The cafeteria doors banged again, and I was starting to get antsy. If Animal Control didn't show up soon, Pompom was gonna hurt herself!

Everybody stared at the doors, uneasy.

Nobody wanted that chicken to get hurt, but nobody wanted to go in and get her either.

I couldn't really see any other way around it.

I couldn't think about it anymore. If I thought about it, then I'd stop myself... so I just did the thing I had to do.

I went into the cafeteria.

EPISODE EIGHTEEN:
POMPOM

152 VIEWS   168 FANS

Yeah... that's what it was like.

Everything was silent.

Like, DEAD SILENT, silent.

Like, all that noise Pompom was making? Gone.

Somehow, that just made it more terrifying. Like, VELOCIRAPTOR levels of terrifying.

Was it possible that I was walking into a trap??

I scanned the cafeteria, but there was no sign of the chicken. Just a bunch of tables with abandoned breakfast food, Pompom's empty chicken coop, and a whole bunch of photography equipment up on the stage for yearbook pictures.

That's when I heard it...

It came from the stage, close to all the photography gear. I heard feathers ruffle, and suddenly, I saw her, perched on a stool like she was about to get her picture taken.

Slowly, I made my way to the stage and slid onto it, acting all casual, not making eye-contact because I didn't want to scare her off.

No answer. Chickens can't talk, but I figured it wouldn't hurt to ask. I kept inching my way toward the stool until I was next to her. Then I reached out slowly, carefully.

Pompom's feathers tickled my fingers as I slid them under her, but... she felt SMALLER than before. Lighter, too... practically weightless, like, whaaat?

I looked down at the thing in my hands. It wasn't Pompom at all, but another one of Evie and Elijah's FAKE chickens!

I heard Evie laugh from outside the cafeteria.

But right at that second, the REAL Pompom must've teleported behind me because she was suddenly RIGHT THERE, clucking with a fury and wildly flapping her wings like some kind of feathered beast!

And I'll tell you this, my friends... I've never NOPE'd out of something so fast in my life. I turned on my heel and started running.

But then, out of the blue, I heard Fergus' voice from the megaphone, not from OUTSIDE the cafeteria, but from INSIDE. He came in to help! In fact, ALL my friends did, Annie, Chuck, and Dutch included!

"Over here!" Fergus shouted, holding Pompom's chicken coop door open. "Get her to chase you over here!"

I ran toward Fergus as fast as I could, but I could practically feel Pompom's beak on my feet. I wasn't sure if I was fast enough, and then my brain had a terrible thought – what if she actually CAUGHT me?

"Death by chicken," wasn't exactly something I wanted on my tombstone.

Pompom was comin' at me like a banshee, so I slid to a stop and turned around. Arms out and eyes closed, I hunkered down, wishing for only ONE thing... please, please, please don't be how I die!

Pompom barreled into me like a train.

I gripped the chonker and masterfully rolled to my feet. She was pecking and scratching at my face while I was screaming and terrified, but I FINALLY had her!

I raced toward Fergus as Annie, Chuck, and Dutch followed, ready to nab the chicken if I dropped her.

FERGUS, GET READY TO CLOSE THE CAGE!

When I was still a few yards away from her chicken coop, Pompom flapped her wings more violently. I had to do something quick or else I was gonna lose my grip on her.

So, I chucked her as hard as I could toward the chicken coop.

She sailed overhead letting out a "BOCAAAAAAWK!" that was probably heard around the world.

I watched as she soared closer to the cage. Closer... closer... until finally...

BAM!

HOLE IN ONE!

Pompom flew inside, Fergus slammed the cage shut, and in the blink of an eye, the whole thing was over. Pompom ruffled her feathers a bit, but then nestled herself back into her home like nothing ever happened.

I dropped to the ground and breathed a much-needed sigh of relief.

At last, Pompom was safe once again.

EPISODE NINETEEN:
WE DID IT!

412 VIEWS   542 FANS

I'm happy to report that the kids at Wood don't hate me anymore! When everybody came back into the cafeteria, I got so many high-fives that my hands went numb.

But don't worry, I made sure that Annie, Chuck, Fergus, and Dutch were also seen as heroes for helping me.

I couldn't have done it without them.

As for Evie, Elijah, Parker, and Chad? They kind of disappeared after, but I'm sure I haven't seen the last of them around... y'know, since they're students at the school, too?

Anyways, the rest of the morning was kind of a blur. The nurse bandaged me up, Animal Control finally got there and gave me a pat on the back, and Principal Davis said I did a great job at saving Pompom without getting her hurt, which was basically his way of saying I'm pretty awesome – his words, not mine.

And after everything settled down, I gave Hawkins my official resignation from the Hall Monitors.

FYI – "resignation" is just a fancy way of saying, "I QUIT!"

Being a Hall Monitor is just too much responsibility, and I've already got enough on my plate with my YouTube videos.

The only problem was that Hawkins wouldn't accept my resignation since I was the CAPTAIN of the Hall Monitors.

Anyways, if I wanted to bail on the job, then I had to choose a NEW Hall Monitor Captain, which wasn't as hard as I thought it'd be.

Annie and Chuck were also done being Hall Monitors, but Fergus wasn't. He offered to be Dutch's second-in-command, so now him and Dutch are living out some kind of buddy cop fantasy, which makes me a teensy bit jealous, but it's cool.

I'll let them have it.

Anyways, after that, me and the gang cleaned up the mess we'd left behind in the cafeteria. And when we were just about done, a line of snazzy lookin' 6th graders came walking through the doors, ready to get their yearbook pictures taken on the stage.

In all the excitement, I had completely forgotten it was picture day for me!

I got in line and waited patiently for my turn. I was scraped up, my hair was a mess, I looked like I just lost a UFC match, and I MIGHT'VE lost a tooth, but I didn't care.

When I was up, the photographer said, "Next!" and I took a seat on the stool. "Okay, smile!"

But I was already smiling.

Best. Yearbook pic. Ever.

And just like every season, I want you (MY AMAZING FANS) to help me figure out what videos to make in the next

DECIDE WHAT HAPPENS
IN THE NEXT Kid YouTuber BOOK!

*YOU'RE ALL COMING UP WITH SOME **AMAZING** IDEAS! AS LONG
AS YOU KEEP SUGGESTING THEM, DAVY WILL KEEP FILMING THEM!
THANK YOU SOOOOO MUCH FOR READING!
YOU. ARE. AWESOME.

‿‿